MW00941314

195 Thoughts Worth Thinking About

By Caleb Hyers

Introduction

"Now, remember, it is I who sends you out,
even though you feel vulnerable as lambs
going into a pack of wolves. So be as
shrewd as snakes yet as harmless as doves."
Matthew 10:16 TPT

I have written this book with the specific
purpose of getting the church thinking again.
I believe that those with the mind of Christ
should be the most brilliant thinkers on the
planet. They should have the wisdom of the
ages flowing from within them. While
intellectualism is not the goal, our minds are
an amazing tool that God has given us to
express the Truth of Christ on the earth.

My hope is not that you agree with
everything written in this book, my hope is
that you take a few moments to think about
what is written. These statements, questions
and thoughts are designed to kickstart the
brain of the Bride of Christ.

There is space on each page where you can
respond with your own thoughts. I
encourage you to disagree, ask questions,

draw something etc... This is designed to be interacted with. So apply each thought and ask good questions about the validity, impact and indications. I see the church rising up and being as shrewd as serpents and gentle as doves. I see the solutions for every problem on the planet coming forth as we access the mind of Christ within us. May the spirit of the living God breathe on your mind as you meditate on these things. Selah.

Truth sent through fire only comes out more true.

In all things, let our relationship with God
be a response to His love.

You will either set culture or culture will set you.

The Church of Jesus Christ should live like
someone died for it.

Wisdom could be simply defined as learning
to love learning.

Its always better to teach others how to think
instead of what to think.

The conclusions you reach are important and so are the ways you reach them.

Passion is the key to any move of God —
and apathy is the killer.

When Love marks your life, no one but the jealous will argue with your methods.

Love isn't fair... and that's ok.

We should stop praying for great people to
come around us and start building them.

Your public worship will always flow from
your private affection.

Disagreement is the atmosphere where
honor is most useful.

God is not against religion, He is against legalism. There is a form of religion that is pure and holy (James 1:27).

Love doesn't call you out, it calls you up to
who you truly are.

The only veil on the Bride of Christ is her eyelids.

Don't swing the sword before you check with the Lord. A word given at the wrong time will only deafen the hearer.

God prefers small faith that never quits over
"big faith" that eventually gives up.

Love will never say, "You are too heavy of a burden."

Love will never say, "You are being too
vulnerable with me."

Love will never say, "You're too much for me to handle."

My theological position is simple: I refuse to elevate the the fall of man above the Cross of Christ.

Delayed obedience is hidden disobedience.

God's first concern is not your behavior, it's your belief.

You can be very wrong in the way that you are right. No matter how right you are.

It takes incredibly more faith to rest than it
does to work.

Needing provision is an agreement with lack. We've already been given all we need.

Sin is not *just* something you can do, its an entity that wants to control you.

Powerful leaders are not "found," they are built.

Sin is an "if-not-when" situation.

You have the power to act outside of your nature but you do not have the power to change it.

I may be your enemy but you are not mine. I don't have any of those.

Seeing a miracle inspires your faith.
Persistence until the point of the miracle
grows it.

Praising your progress will always do more to motivate you then focusing on your failures.

A healthy relationship is the wineskin of wisdom. God imparts revelation knowledge through the people closest to you.

A wise man trusts the wisdom of his friends.

If you walked in on Jesus hanging out with your worst enemy, would you stay in the room?

Jesus is the only way to see God, the Old
Testament, and the future correctly.

The next time you negatively judge someone
for the company they keep, consider the
company Christ kept.

Many believe this lie: I must work the rest of my life to get the rest of Heaven. The truth is we enter into rest as soon as we believe its available.

Of all God has given us, our words hold the most power to create. The Creator Himself is the Word.

We are not saved to sit, but we are saved to rest.

We are called to "be holy" as He is holy,
therefore Holiness is a state of being, not a
state of doing.

The church is waiting for Jesus to come back but Jesus is waiting for the church to come out.

Forgiveness is the essence of Godliness.

God doesn't wait until the last moment, God
waits until the moment of trust.

I disagree with the lie that a *lifestyle* of peace is abnormal for the believer.

Fact informs while truth inspires.

You create worlds with your words. Create
wisely.

Find me someone who Perfect Love would not be friends with. That's the only person you are allowed to hate.

You cannot earn that which is free and the
Gospel is called a gift.

With Jesus, perceived distance is only an
invitation into the waters of deeper
relationship.

We are not motivated by the law of God, we are motivated by the Love of God.

The Gospel of the Kingdom is about Heaven
coming to earth, not you going to heaven.

You can not hope to regulate a relationship
with an irregular Holy Spirit.

A melody can carry the entire cosmos. It's called the Uni-verse.

If you humble yourself to learn from anyone, almost anyone will learn from you.

Learning to lose well is necessary to
maintain success when it comes.

You're not becoming more holy. You're becoming more aware of Christ's holiness within you.

If you have to use your title or credentials to win an argument, you have most likely lost.

Sin pays a wage but God gives a gift!
Eternal life.

Taking responsibility for your actions is simply recognizing your ability to respond.

Our war is not against flesh and blood;
therefore you are not your own worst enemy.

It is totally possible to teach from the Bible and not teach the Gospel at the same exact time.

If you think that you do not have time, then
time actually has you.

To hate wisdom is to love death. To love
wisdom is to welcome correction for life.

The only appropriate approach to spiritual
warfare is found in the life of Jesus.

Brokenness, though the starting point, is not the norm for the Believer. Victory is.

Your capacity for holiness has everything to
do with Christ *in* you.

God became man so that men could become
like God again.

If the believer sins, the reaction should be,
"That is so un-like you!"

Success in the Kingdom of God is measured
by obedience, not results.

God is more patient with you than you are.

I don't need to be right, I need to know the truth.

True family always fights for connection.

Faith is what connects hope and action. It always takes you somewhere.

The world will only go to Hell in a hand
basket if the church hides under one.

Ask yourself, "How can I add value to the
people around me today?"

The fool shuts his ears to critique but
Wisdom asks for feedback.

Learn how to give and you will have learned
the nature of God.

If your solution isn't redemptive, then you
do not have God's solution.

The storms in your life should be more
affected by you than you are by them.

Gratitude will never look bad on you.

The Christian life starts from union with Christ, not for it.

Never fear being great, fear making others
feel like they are not.

We must remain teachable or dare not teach at all.

Refusing to learn is the essence of pride.

I'm not going to get offended, because you have to 'take offense,' and I'm not taking that.

Eternity in heaven is great. Eternal life is better. One is a future hope and the other is our present reality.

The Cross of Jesus Christ is the first kiss of
the new covenant.

Any theology that teaches you should still
expect to sin is, in fact, a sin.

Humility comes before honor and dishonor
paves the way for pride.

The bonds of honor are not truly tested until everything goes wrong.

If you want to see miracles, go where they
are necessary.

This moment is the most important moment because it is the only moment you are ever in.

The secret of contentedness is the gaze of
Jesus Christ.

A "mighty move of God" cannot be the
point, Jesus must be the point.

We do not need to receive more faith. We simply need to persist in the faith we have.

Jesus came in the line of Adam in order to
end the line of Adam. (See Romans 5:12-21)

When you dishonor someone it speaks more
of you then it does them.

We stand on every word God has said and
we step with every word God is saying.

We do not honor people because of who they are, we honor others because of who we are.

There was once a man who having learned
all things was more ignorant than any.

"Forward thinking" requires present awareness.

When the past matters more than the present
you build monuments instead of movements.

They "why" behind your "what" is what's
most important.

Pray for patience — its the first thing Love
is.

The Gospel will never be about what we do
for God but what Christ did for us.

In the Kingdom of God, we give so that we
can give even more.

The ongoing revelation of Christ and Him crucified is the only revelation you will ever need.

Our communication must be measured by
the understanding it imparts, not merely the
intent with which it is sent.

Recognizing sin doesn't welcome condemnation, it invites reconciliation.

Don't fight the enemy, take a victory lap.
Christ has overcome the world.

Worry is the worship language of Hell.

It takes a virgin bride to carry the seed of
Christ. And you are the Bride of Christ.

The seat of service becomes the throne of destiny. Take the low place.

The world is starving for the supernatural
and the Church should be feeding them.

Refuse to preach the gospel without a demonstration of God's goodness and power.

You can't spell "wrestle" without "rest." You will win more if you rest more.

Believing in God is great. Believing what
God believes about you is better.

If it all fits in your head, its too small to be God.

Christianity is not an ideology, it's a supernatural encounter with a person called Love.

Your emotions are no substitute for the Holy Ghost. Let God guide your decisions.

Just because you feel it, doesn't mean you are it.

Spiritual hunger is a gift from God. You should feel it when you don't eat well.

You will always look like what you look at.

Our union with Christ must be the
cornerstone of our identity.

Bridal affection is the highest form of worship.

Truth does not drop from your head to your heart. It starts in the deepest places of you and bubbles up from there.

Our intellect does not inform our spirit, our spirit informs our intellect so we need not lean on our own understanding.

Here's some good news: you have one
source and it is not you.

Thanksgiving *before* your breakthrough is played on the loudspeaker of hell.

To be seated in heavenly places means
you're able to see from heaven's
perspective.

Hope and hype are entirely different. One presses you forward, the other leaves you depressed.

Some captives boast they are free while they are not, and some who are free boast they are captives.

What if every time you where tempted you told the devil who you are?

Searching for gold in others means you have to dig. Staring at dirt keeps everyone poor.

God has done amazing things and will do amazing things but more importantly, God is doing amazing things.

God does not call Himself the "I Was" or the
"I Will Be." He is the "I Am."

Living for Christ is good. Living from Him
is better.

The effects of Salvation are immediate and eternal at the same time.

Sanctification is a one-time event.
Revelation of that sanctification is the
process.

The result of worshipping your efforts and creations is union with the spirit of idolatry.

.

The next time you read your Bible, expect to encounter the Author.

Maybe if the Church was happier the world would listen to what we have to say.

God laughs every time the devil schemes.
Be like God.

Joy is a violent weapon of hope.

The beauty lost in the fall of man was given back in the ascension of Christ. So walk in your beauty.

Jesus did more than pay for my sin, He set
me free from my sin-struggle.

Joy is a third of the Kingdom that we are supposed to be praying would come to earth.

False humility is the most dangerous form of
pride.

Humility requires greatness. It's impossible to be humble about accomplishing nothing.

"Knowledge" without the Spirit of Wisdom
is dangerous.

The Bible is more than a moral code, it is an expression of a living being.

I don't need my own opinion when I have a
book full of God's thoughts about me.

True righteousness is attractive. Jesus
always had a crowd.

Don't strive to be more patient. Patience is
the fruit of union with an eternal being. It
will grow naturally the longer you abide in
Christ.

If you need everything in one moment you
will miss the hour.

If you lead but refuse to learn you will only
lead others into ignorance.

Everything I was died with Christ on the cross. Everything I am now is in Him.

Jesus died *for* you and Jesus died *as* you.

A true sign of maturity is the ability to admit your mistakes with grace.

Everything God does is in the context of relationship. Intimacy is always God's goal.

Righteousness is a gift. You walk *in* righteousness when you walk in intimacy with the Giver.

Peace is not something you have, its
Someone who has you.

Joy is not something you do, its a fruit that you bear.

Creativity happens best in community
because the Creator is a community.

"Satisfaction" is the Kingdom of God looks
like hunger.

Love matures you by forgetting your faults.

The Cross of Christ revealed God's value for you.

If you need to do something in order to receive freedom, then it is not a gift from God.

We are not completing an unfinished work.
We are believing the completely finished
work of Christ.

Salvation didn't just happen for you, it
happened to you.

While it's not impossible for a Christian to sin, it should be highly improbable.

To fear disagreement is to fear growth and to love disagreement is to stunt growth.

Gratitude will always clean the lens of your attitude so you can see clearly.

Love is my Master. I have no time to obey
the requests of the evil one.

Without the lens of love, you cannot see the
Kingdom of God.

The process of yielding to mystery is essential knowledge.

Speaking the truth in love is not the same as loving to speak what is true.

It is nearly impossible to say anything
without offending someone.

All of God's paths for His children require
going *with* Him.

Keep your head in the clouds and your feet on the ground, you're big enough for both.

If your version of truth results in fear, guilt,
or bondage — it is not the Gospel.

It is impossible to represent the God of love
while preaching hate.

When you demonize a person, you forfeit
the ministry of reconciliation.

Be careful that your opinions don't rob you
of the opportunity to love.

Just be you. It's the only thing nobody else
can do.

Passion is not a personality type.

If the Gospel does not penetrate every part
of your person then it is only partially good
news.

Let me hear how you speak about others and
I will show you how you feel about yourself.

The Love of God is both a firm foundation
and a bottomless sea.

When the enemy says you're unqualified,
take it as a compliment. All he can do is lie.

Any lack of forgiveness toward someone is simply unbelief in the finished work of Christ.

Fear is nothing but faith pointed in the
wrong direction.

Made in the USA
Monee, IL
24 November 2019

17341164R00116